DINOSAURS

By Steve Parker
Illustrated by Chris Buzer

Miles Kelly
PUBLISHING

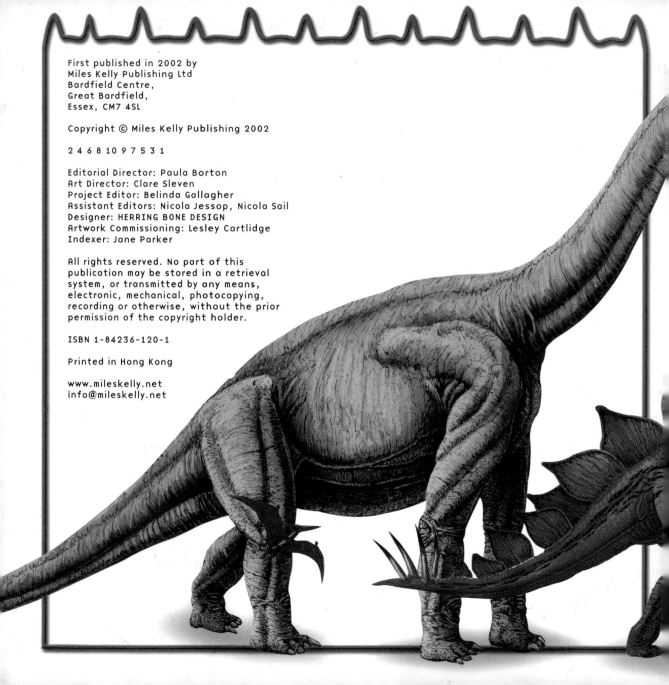

First published in 2002 by
Miles Kelly Publishing Ltd
Bardfield Centre,
Great Bardfield,
Essex, CM7 4SL

2 4 6 8 10 9 7 5 3 1

Editorial Director: Paula Borton
Art Director: Clare Sleven
Project Editor: Belinda Gallagher
Assistant Editors: Nicola Jessop, Nicola Sail
Designer: HERRING BONE DESIGN
Artwork Commissioning: Lesley Cartlidge
Indexer: Jane Parker

ISBN 1-84236-120-1

Printed in Hong Kong

www.mileskelly.net
Info@mileskelly.net

Contents

1 King of the dinosaurs

Dinosaur facts

- Tyrannosaurus was 12 metres in length.
- It lived in North America.
- It was one of the last dinosaurs and lived about 65 million years ago.

Dinosaur name

- Say it: 'Ty-ran-owe-saw-rus-rex'.

- It means 'king of the tyrant lizards'.

TYRANNOSAURUS REX was one of the biggest hunting animals ever to walk the Earth. This massive meat-eater had more than 50 teeth — each one of them was bigger than your hand.

Tyrannosaurus weighed about seven tonnes — that's as heavy as two elephants.

The teeth of Tyrannosaurus had wavy, saw-like edges called serrations. They could easily slice through the flesh of its victim.

Even bigger!
Giganotosaurus was another meat-eating dinosaur. It was even larger than Tyrannosaurus!

The arms of Tyrannosaurus were tiny and probably useless.

5

Hammer-tailed dinosaur!

Dinosaur facts

- Ankylosaurus lived 70 million years ago in North America.
- It was 10 metres long and weighed five tonnes.

Dinosaur name

- Say it: 'An-kill-owe-saw-rus'.
- It means 'stiff or fused lizard'.

ANKYLOSAURUS had two heavy lumps of bone at the end of its tail. It could swing these at enemies like a huge hammer. But for most of the time, this dinosaur was a peaceful plant-eater.

Ankylosaurus was protected by long spikes of bone on its head and shoulders.

Each lump of bone on the tail was as big as a basketball.

Bony tail

The tail club of *Ankylosaurus* was made of bone, which had become stuck, or fused, together.

Pieces of bone as big as dinner plates, and very hard scales, protected the back of Ankylosaurus.

Ankylosaurus crouched down to protect its soft underside.

Dinosaur facts

• Deinonychus was 1.6 metres high – as tall as a human.
• It lived in North America 110 million years ago.

Dinosaur name

• Say it: 'Day-non-ee-cuss'.
• It means 'terrible claw'.

DEINONYCHUS went on the prowl in a group or pack. In this way it could attack prey much bigger than itself, like a one-tonne *Tenontosaurus*. This gave enough food for a whole week!

Some dinosaurs died and their bones, teeth and claws were preserved as fossils. The fossils of several Deinonychus were found together, showing that they lived and hunted in groups.

Deinonychus *had strong back legs. It could run fast, jump high and leap a long way.*

Clever dinosaur?

The brain of Deinonychus was quite big compared to other dinosaurs. It may have been pretty clever!

Deinonychus *slashed out with its powerful hand claws.*

The toe of Deinonychus had a huge, curved claw. This was used to rip open its victim.

Plate-backed dinosaur

Dinosaur facts

• Stegosaurus lived about 150 million years ago in North America.
• Stegosaurus was nine metres long and weighed two tonnes.

Dinosaur name

• Say it: Steg-owe-sore-uss'.
• It means 'roof lizard'.

STEGOSAURUS had tall, thin plates of bone on its back. Why? Perhaps they soaked up the Sun's heat, to make this dinosaur warm. The hotter *Stegosaurus* got, the faster it moved.

Stegosaurus had a mouth shaped like a bird's beak, for pecking at plant food.

The back plates were as tall and wide as a pillow. But they were only as thick as your wrist.

Tiny brain

Stegosaurus was as big as an elephant, but its brain was as small as your thumb. So it wasn't very clever!

Caring mother

Dinosaur facts
- Maiasaura was nine metres in length.
- It lived 80 million years ago in North America.

Dinosaur name
- Say it: 'My-ah-sore-ah'.
- It means 'good mother lizard'.

The big plant-eating dinosaur **MAIASAURA** laid its eggs in a bowl-shaped nest, which it scooped in the soil. It protected the eggs from hungry enemies and even fed the babies when they hatched.

Fossils have been found of Maiasaura nests, babies and grown-ups. The nests were quite close together, in a group called a breeding colony.

The Maiasaura nest was about two metres across and contained around 20 eggs.

Each baby Maiasaura hatched from an egg about as big as your two fists placed end-to-end. Its leg bones were not quite strong enough for it to run around.

The mother Maiasaura brought leaves and berries back to the nest, for her babies to eat.

Mega eggs!

Some mother dinosaurs laid eggs 30 centimetres long – the size of a rugby ball – and as big as 50 hen's eggs.

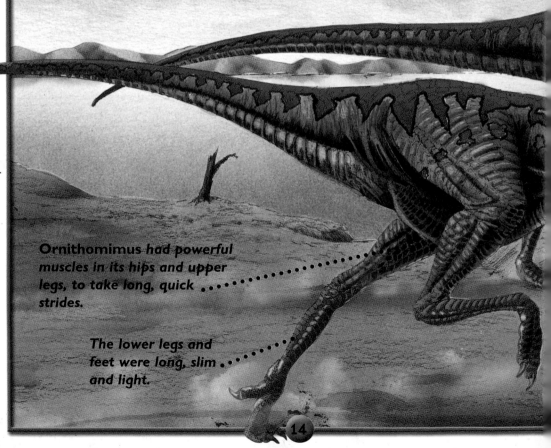

6 Speedy dinosaurs

Fast-running dinosaurs like **ORNITHOMIMUS** were called 'ostrich-dinosaurs'. This is because they were very similar in size and shape to the bird of today, the ostrich. Perhaps they ran as fast, too!

Dinosaur facts

• Ornithomimus was about three metres long and lived 75 million years ago.

Dinosaur name

• Say it: 'Or-nith-owe-mim-uss'.
• It means 'like an ostrich'.

Ornithomimus had powerful muscles in its hips and upper legs, to take long, quick strides.

The lower legs and feet were long, slim and light.

The long neck of Ornithomimus helped it to peck on the ground. ··············

Ornithomimus had no teeth at all! Its long, beak-shaped mouth was suited to pecking and snapping up all kinds of foods, from leaves to little lizards.

Fastest!

An ostrich-dinosaur or an ostrich would not quite catch the fastest runner today – the cheetah.

Ornithomimus had a top speed of 80 kilometres an hour – twice as fast as a champion human sprinter.

The plant-eater **PARASAUROLOPHUS** had a long tube of bone sticking up from the back of its head. This was hollow. Perhaps the dinosaur blew air through it to make loud noises — just like an elephant does when it 'trumpets' through its trunk.

Perhaps Parasaurolophus made noises to frighten off enemies. These noises may have helped to attract a mate, or warned other herd members of danger.

Dinosaur facts

• Parasauro-lophus lived 70 million years ago in North America.

• It was 10 metres from nose to tail.

Dinosaur name

• Say it: 'Pa-ra-sore-owe-loaf-uss'.

• It means 'beside ridged lizard'.

Dino-song!

Roll a card sheet into a long tube. Shout and make noises through it. Maybe that's how dinosaurs 'sang'!

Parasaurolophus breathed air in through its nose. The air passed up and down inside the hollow tube, before it went into the body.

The bony tube had no hole at the end. Its tip was sealed.

8 Dinosaur giant!

BRACHIOSAURUS was one of the biggest dinosaurs that ever lived. It weighed over 50 tonnes — more than a huge juggernaut truck. It was also one of the tallest dinosaurs. Its head could stretch to 13 metres above the ground.

Dinosaur facts
- Brachiosaurus was 25 metres in length.
- It lived 140 million years ago in Africa, Europe and North America.

Dinosaur name
- Say it: 'Brack-ee-owe-sore-uss'.
- It means 'arm lizard'.

Giant feet!

Brachiosaurus had huge feet and made footprints one metre across — bigger than a school desk.

Because of its huge size, *Brachiosaurus* must have spent its whole life eating. Its neck was more than eight metres long, the same length as a flag pole!

Brachiosaurus had a small head and peg-like teeth for pulling leaves off twigs.

The front legs, or 'arms', were longer than the back legs, adding to the great height of *Brachiosaurus*.

19

Dinosaur facts

• Compsog-nathus lived 150 million years ago in Europe.

Dinosaur name

• Say it: 'Comp-sog-nay-thuss'.
• It means 'elegant jaw'.

COMPSOGNATHUS was just about the tiniest dinosaur. However, even though it was small, it was very fierce. *Compsognathus* was a speedy hunter of little creatures such as insects, worms — and perhaps baby dinosaurs.

Compsognathus was small and slender. It weighed only three kilograms — less than an average pet cat.

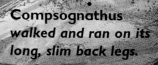

Compsognathus *walked and ran on its long, slim back legs.*

The head on the long, bendy neck could dart about and snap up prey.

Compsognathus had many small, sharp, curved teeth for biting its tiny victims.

The arms of Compsognathus had sharp claws for grabbing food.

Micro dino!

Compsognathus was about as tall as a chicken of today, but much thinner — and without the feathers.

H97108

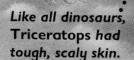

Dinosaur horns and frills

Dinosaur facts
- Triceratops lived 65 million years ago.
- It was nine metres long and weighed five tonnes.

Dinosaur name
- Say it 'Try-sarah-tops'.
- It means 'three horns on the face'.

TRICERATOPS was usually a quiet, peaceful plant-eater. But if an enemy came near, it charged with its head down, and jabbed with its long, sharp horns. The wide frill of bone over its neck made it look even more fearsome!

Like all dinosaurs, Triceratops had tough, scaly skin.

Triceratops *had to defend itself against the great meat-eater* Tyrannosaurus. *These two dinosaurs lived at the same time in the same region.*

Shadow dino!

Put your fingers in the positions shown, between a desk lamp and the wall. See the shadowy dinosaur!

The nose horn of Triceratops *was quite short. But the horns over the eyes were more than one metre long.*

Index